CHANGE AGENT

CHANGE AGENT

One Person's Journey from Traditional to Biblical Christianity

DANIEL MOYNIHAN

WinePress Publishing
Great Books, Defined.

WinePress Publishing is honored to present this title in partnership with the author. The views expressed or implied in this work are those of the author. WinePress provides our imprint seal representing design excellence, creative content and high quality production. To learn more about Responsible Publishing™ visit www.winepresspublishing.com.

ISBN 13: 978-1-4141-2550-3
ISBN 10: 1-4141-2550-X
Library of Congress Catalog Card Number: 2013900381

Dedicated to my fellow change agent,
Kathy; our kids, Danielle, Debbie, Kristin,
Stephen; and our grandkids

CONTENTS

FOREWORD

THIS BOOK IS by no means a biography. If it were, there would be numerous stories about the great times I have spent with my wonderful wife, kids, and grandkids. There would be details about my good times and tough times. It is interesting, but not something you would feel compelled to write a book about. What I did feel compelled to write about is the story of how my changed theological perspective altered the theological perspective of my family. I hope my children and their children continue along this new path. If they do, future generations will look back and see how a long history of traditional Catholicism was suddenly altered and changed to biblical Christianity by the grace of God in my lifetime.

This can sound rather self-serving, but I don't mean it to be so. I give all the credit to God. I thank Him for giving me an inquisitive mind. I thank Him for putting people and situations in my path that gave me the answers I was seeking and the convictions I needed to effect change in my life and in the life of my family. Some people will see this book as a knock on Catholicism. It is not meant to be that. There are many people in that church system who love the Lord and are able to serve Him there despite the many disadvantages I found within it myself.

The term "change agent" has been used in various ways over the past few years. If you look for a definition online you will see it usually described in conjunction with a business, whereby someone has altered the mindset of the direction of a company. He or she has done so by altering the way things are done and/or the philosophy of how things are/will be done. I call myself a change agent because I see how God has used me to alter and change the mindset of my family's theological thinking.

This book concentrates on the specific events and situations that affected me as I went from being born into traditional Catholicism to becoming a minister in a nondenominational Bible-believing Christian church. Part 1 of the book details the events that happened in my life as I became a change agent. Part 2 details my thoughts and insights.

Whenever I have taught on any theological topic, I have told my students to not just take what I was saying as absolute. I have always taught that they should verify what I was teaching for themselves. When you do this, what you believe is more firmly grounded because you know why you believe what you believe—you don't believe it just because you heard it somewhere. So many people are raised in one system or another and simply believe it because it is what they were taught. Well, one can be raised being taught that gravity is not a real concept. Step off of a tall building and you will find out that you were taught incorrectly. Build your house on the rock, not the sand. Take the necessary time to study these topics for yourself, so you will be able to withstand any storms that may come your way.

Part One

A CHANGE AGENT'S JOURNEY

Chapter 1

WHO WILL ANSWER?

> But sanctify the Lord God in your hearts, and always be ready to give a defense to everyone who asks you a reason for the hope that is in you.
>
> —1 Peter 3:15

"IF JESUS DIED on the cross for us, why do we have to pay for our sins in purgatory?" At fourteen years old I asked this question of a Catholic nun who was teaching a religion class. This was one of many religious questions troubling me as I entered my teen years. The look of confusion and exasperation on her face was quite enlightening.

"What made you think to ask that?" she said. "Just accept what the Holy Father and saints of the church have told us for centuries. Who are we to question?" It was as if she had never thought of this herself, and the idea that she had no answer whatsoever flustered her.

This was typical of questions I asked during my middle school years of various Catholic teachers or my parents. I asked my father similar questions one day. His response was similar to the nun's.

"The leaders of the church had been around for a long time, so they must have it right," he said.

These types of answers seemed to be telling me to believe what I was taught and shut up. However, I had an inquisitive mind, and I was not going to stop asking difficult questions. I just did not know anybody who could provide me with answers. Some people can just shrug their shoulders when they have such questions and accept it and go on, while others start to fade away from their belief system. Even at a young age, I just wanted to know the truth. This was not the norm. Most kids I knew didn't have the same questions. I was convinced that the Catholicism I was raised in was right (how could it not be?) and that the "evil" Protestant line of thinking was wrong. I just did not understand how and why Catholicism was right and Protestantism was wrong.

My parents loved my two sisters and me. However they had both been raised in the standard generic Catholicism. It suited them both well. They had no issues with it that I can remember. They were born into it and did not question it. Catholicism was right and everything else was wrong. It had been that way in our family as far back as anybody could remember. It was the typical type of North American Catholicism in which they knew a lot about Catholic church doctrine and the latest thing the pope had to say, but very little about the Bible or general things about God.

We never had any discussions on theological matters that I can remember. Catholics were right and all Protestant denominations were wrong and likely doomed. They showed no interest when movies such as Charlton Heston's *Ten Commandments* came on television at Easter every year. Neither did any of my Catholic friends. They went to church because their parents made them. No one wanted to talk about God when I brought the subject up. I am sure that is not the case in all Catholic families, but that was my experience.

There were so many things I did not understand. I was one of the few kids I knew who actually liked going to church (not that I had a choice). However I was constantly confused. I liked the two epistle readings (usually one short chapter from the Old Testament and one short chapter from one of the New Testament). Then there would be a short gospel reading from Matthew, Mark, Luke, or John. I liked the readings, but sometimes they (especially the

Old Testament ones) were difficult to understand. No one ever explained what they were about. Other than the readings, the rest of the Mass was repetitive prayers or sayings, so that got boring. I had some friends who became ushers just so they could be doing something to pass the time.

I really wanted to know who Jesus was. When the Shroud of Turin was big news I took the picture of what was being called the real face of Jesus and cut it out to put into a frame. I reasoned that if this was the real face of Jesus, then that is what I wanted hanging in my room—not a bunch of statues that made no sense to me. My parents placed a statue in my room of Jesus as an infant with royal robes. But from what I understood the infant Jesus never wore such robes. He was born in a humble stable to poor folks. Yes, He was divine, but as an infant, He never wore such robes, so it all seemed fake to me.

Along with the purgatory question, I still could not understand or find anyone who could answer the following questions:

- Is there really a God? How can we know?
- Why do good people suffer?
- Are the Bible stories such as Adam and Eve, Noah's ark, and Jonah and the fish just stories or did they really happen?

- Why did God create different races? How could everyone come from one couple given that we all look so different?
- If God is all powerful and wants us to know Him, why are there so many religions and different kinds of churches?
- Is there any proof that Jesus rose from the dead?
- Why was I born? What is my purpose?

Throughout my teen years, I struggled with these and many other unanswered questions as I shuffled off to Catholic Mass. It was not until my junior year in high school that something significant occurred. I had a job in a mall near home at Baskin Robbins. One night while closing the store, I was surrounded (the ice cream store was in the middle of the mall and set up as a kiosk) by Bible-toting college students. Worse than mainline Protestants, these were the "born-again Christians." Technically they were Protestants, but at the time they were considered their own radical group by what was considered mainstream because they dared to evangelize others to their way of thinking.

"Are you saved?" one of them asked me.

"Would you go to heaven if you died tonight?" another asked.

On and on the questions went, but since I had a lot of unanswered questions in my own mind, I certainly could not come close to answering theirs. I knew enough Catholic doctrine to fake my way through their onslaught in a convincing fashion, but as I walked home that night, I was more troubled than ever.

Their convictions were much stronger than mine. They had answers and convictions in their beliefs, I had none. Worse yet, I had no one to talk to. My parents didn't have any answers. The church didn't have any answers. And my friends were clueless and uninterested. I had a hard time taking Catholicism seriously as a result.

I had friends and relatives who were afraid to miss Mass (in the Catholic faith, it is a mortal sin to miss Mass without a real good excuse). But then I would hear them make racial slurs and they would insult others. It seemed quite inconsistent with what I would glean from Scripture readings during Mass. Now, no one is perfect and we all struggle with our various vices. But I did not see any struggle. That's what bothered me.

For many of the Catholics I knew (certainly not all), it seemed like their religion was either a part-time thing or they were allowed to ignore the doctrines they disagreed with. When Catholicism started the practice of shaking hands with your neighbor during the Mass, some were infuriated. "What if I can't stand the person behind me?" I would hear. From some of the gospel and epistle readings I would hear that we were to love and forgive one another. From what I could see, too many were ignoring these commands. If we were going to ignore what we were being taught, what was the point in going to church?

I began to drift away during my high school years. I attended church simply because I had to. I would occasionally get something out of the readings, as I used to, but for the most part I was bored stiff. Without answers to my questions, it all seemed like meaningless ritual. I knew there was a God. There were occasions when I would ask Him to reveal Himself to me. I told Him I really wanted to know the truth about Him. When you are sincere and speak that way, He will answer. Nothing could prepare me for the way He decided to answer.

Points to Ponder

1. Do you believe your theology simply because it is the belief system you were raised in?
2. How important is it to have a firm foundation for your beliefs?

Chapter 2

SALTWATER BAPTISM

> But now, thus says the LORD, who created you, O Jacob, And He who formed you, O Israel: "Fear not, for I have redeemed you; I have called *you* by your name; You *are* Mine. When you pass through the waters, I *will* be with you; And through the rivers, they shall not overflow you.
>
> Isaiah 43:1–2

FOLLOWING HIGH SCHOOL I joined the U.S. Coast Guard. I had applied for West Point but was not selected. Joining the Coast Guard was my back up plan. I joined the Coast Guard right after graduation from high school. During the first year and a half, I stopped going to Catholic Mass. I still considered myself a Catholic, but without answers, my convictions regarding Catholic doctrine had started to wane. I firmly believed in God, but was still not sure how to go about knowing more about Him. In my third year with the Coast Guard I was transferred to a ship in Kodiak, Alaska. I met two guys onboard who would become influential in my thinking. One worked at the land base there and the other one on the ship.

They were both born-again Christians, but of a different sort. They didn't shout at me or pepper me with questions. Their calm and strong spirit made them approachable. When they spoke, I wanted to listen. They had been raised as Christians, and they went to church, but they considered their relationship with Christ to be more important than the church they attended. This was totally foreign to me.

Out at sea we didn't have much to do at night. People say not to discuss religion or politics, but bored sailors will talk about anything. One night, ten or twelve of us were sitting around and arguing about religion. My calm Christian shipmate was on duty so he was not a part of this. I was losing my Catholic convictions, so I was not a part of the argument. I just listened. It allowed me to observe something fascinating. The four Catholic guys were defending their point of view and why they were right. The Lutheran guy was defending his way. So was the Methodist guy, the Presbyterian guy, and the agnostic guy. As I listened, it became obvious that everyone was defending his point of view from the way he was raised. None of them had any strong arguments, convictions, or reasons for their point of view.

Truth seemed to have nothing to do with their arguments. It dawned on me that if the Methodist guy had been raised Presbyterian, he would be defending that path. If the Lutheran guy had been raised Methodist, he would be defending that path. I realized right then and there that if my parents had both been any one of those, then that is what I would be trying to defend as well.

I had always been an avid reader, and even more so when I was assigned to the ship. Not having much to do at sea, books were always a good escape. In late November 1979, I went into the Kodiak Bookstore to get three or four books for an upcoming sea mission, including *The Late Great Planet Earth* by Hal Lindsey. I did not fully realize it was a book about spiritual matters. It had a snazzy title and was being touted as a huge bestseller. I started reading it that night and could not put it down. It began to answer many of my questions.

Lindsey answered the question about why Jesus was the way, rather than other gods such as Buddha and Muhammad. He didn't stress church or denomination, but instead he stressed the importance of where you stood with Jesus. For the first time in my life I understood why Jesus had to come to earth to die for us. Lindsey pointed out that the animal sacrifices the Israelites performed were a temporary covering of sin. These sacrifices pointed forward to the Messiah, who would be the ultimate Lamb of God who would take away the sin of the world. The Israelites looked forward to the cross, while we look back to it.

Beyond all that, Lindsey introduced me to Bible prophecy, saying Jesus was most likely coming back in my generation. And he went into great detail about why. In the Catholic church we chanted during every Mass: "Christ has died, Christ is risen, Christ will come again." The problem is no one ever spoke about when or how He was coming again. Lindsey's book did, and it intrigued me to no end.

At the end of the book he included a sinner's prayer. Lindsey's prayer spoke of receiving Jesus as Lord and Savior of your life. While my biblical knowledge was growing, I still had a lot to learn. One thing I did know—I wanted to know this Jesus more than anything, so I said the prayer. I reasoned that once I got out of the Coast Guard, I would have the chance to understand this even more, but it turned out that I didn't have long to wait.

On the morning of December 5, 1979, I got into a small lifeboat with a fellow crew member named Mike to deliver some batteries to a beacon tower out in the Alaska Aleutian island chain. After traveling several miles from the safety of our 180-foot mother ship, a vicious storm came up (which is common in the Alaska Bering Sea). As we were nearing the beacon, a rogue wave came up behind us and flipped our small boat. I was immediately sucked underwater. Mike was as well, but he quickly washed up on the rock, grabbing onto the rocks near the beacon tower. From his point of view, I was gone. He said later he saw my gloves and boots floating on the churning sea, but no sign of me anywhere.

What happened to me was surreal, but I will explain it the best I can. As the boat flipped, the waves tore it apart. I tried to cling to part of it but was pulled underwater by the suction of the undertow. Even after all these years, I can still remember the intense pain of the cold water, which I had heard about but never experienced. I was sucked down ten to twelve feet below the surface. I tried to swim to the surface, but my legs and arms were so numb from the frigid water that I could hardly move them.

After I could hold my breath no longer, water began to fill my mouth and lungs. One moment I was in extreme pain from drowning, thinking about my family back home, and the next moment I felt no pain. It did not matter that I could not breathe. I felt myself separate from my physical body and I felt like I was floating toward something warm and peaceful. At the same time I felt like I was in the presence of something or someone wonderful.

I can't explain it any more than that. To me it seemed like seconds. Mike said I was gone about twenty minutes. I reentered my body and at that moment all the pain returned. Something pushed me up to the surface. Once I reached it, I floated on my back for some time, and then a wave pushed me toward Mike, which was a miracle in itself considering the raging sea. We huddled there for thirty hours until we were found and rescued by a Coast Guard helicopter. We were near death from hypothermia. While we waited for the possibility of rescue, we wondered if we were going to make it—if they would find us in the storm and be able to rescue us in time. But because of the strange thing that happened to me underwater, I somehow knew I was going to live.

I prayed the sinner's prayer the night before. Looking back on that now, I have no doubt that Christ saved my soul the moment I uttered the prayer. I intended to learn more about my relationship with Him later, but the very next day, He got my attention through my baptism in salt water.

Points to Ponder

1. It took a traumatic experience for me to get serious about understanding the truth about God. Is God reaching out to you today so you will follow and understand Him more closely? You don't have to wait for a life-threatening experience. He wants you to follow Him right now.
2. Can you defend what you believe or are you parroting what you were taught, with no confidence in your understanding?

Chapter 3

PROGRESSIVE CHANGE

My son, if you receive my words, And treasure my commands within you, So that you incline your ear to wisdom, *And* apply your heart to understanding; Yes, if you cry out for discernment, *And* lift up your voice for understanding, If you seek her as silver, And search for her as for hidden treasures; Then you will understand the fear of the LORD, And find the knowledge of God.

—Proverbs 2:1–5

AFTER OUR AMAZING rescue we were taken to the Kodiak Hospital in Kodiak, Alaska. I will always be grateful to the men who flew the rescue helicopter in gale-force winds. I never did have the opportunity to meet them. Mike was released after a couple of days after treatment for hypothermia. I was in the hospital for five weeks.

I had been in the thirty-two-degree water for at least twenty minutes with my bare feet because my boots had gotten sucked off as I was pulled underwater. Then came the thirty hours of exposure. My feet were black upon rescue. The doctor aboard the rescue helicopter said he thought I would lose my feet. Doctors were able to treat, and ultimately save, my feet, but I have a permanent disability to this day called "frozen feet." It means I have nerve damage to the interior of my feet, so they tire easily and get cold quickly. It's inconvenient, but it's better than the alternative.

While stuck in the hospital, I asked my buddies to go to the town bookstore to buy any other Hal Lindsey books they could find. They brought me *There is a New World Coming* and *Satan is Alive and Well on Planet Earth*. I devoured both books. And then a hospital chaplain gave me a Bible. In the past, I had trouble understanding the Bible, but something had changed. I had a new level of understanding and ability to grasp what I could not before. I attribute it to what happened to me underwater. Ever since that moment of which I was out of my body and connected to something warm and wonderful, I have had a passion to read and study the Bible and books related to it. I believe the Lord gave me a type of gift of understanding, as things just came more easily to me. Ephesians 3:1–5 tells us that the Lord gives all believers the ability to understand the Bible through the Holy Spirit. I have been told that when I teach I make difficult things easy to understand. I can't brag about that any more than a good athlete can brag about his or her gift. It comes from God, and we are responsible to use it.

As I was reading and studying in the hospital, it became clear to me what I had to do if I were going to seek real truth and get all my questions answered, at least as much as they can be answered in this life. I needed to take everything I had been taught about Jesus and Christianity in general and start over. I had to go back to the teachings of Jesus and the apostles at the time of the early church and go from there. If I started back when the church began and went through history to the present, I could understand how all of the Christian denominations came to be—and why. I had to learn to "eat the meat and spit out the bones," meaning I needed to learn and accept what was taught by God and not necessarily what was added by the whims of man. Now, if the man was inspired by God, OK. But too often that is not the case.

After the five-week hospital stay in Alaska, I was transferred to a Coast Guard base in Manhattan, New York. Talk about culture shock! Facing a long road to recovery, I spent half the day in physical therapy and the other half in a Coast Guard base office. The best part was that Manhattan was full of Christian bookstores. My library of books quickly grew. Whatever the Lord had imparted to me would not stop, as I felt the drive to keep studying and learning. I also started to watch some preachers on TV. Some annoyed me as I discerned their lack of sincerity and eagerness to make money. Some were magnificent and helped my understanding grow. One was Dr. Charles Stanley. It did not matter how long he spoke, he took the Scriptures and made them come alive.

I also had a new appreciation for Christian music. I could not believe there were actually record albums and eight-track tapes (yes, this was a long time ago) that were totally devoted to praising Jesus and about living the Christian life. Visiting Christian book- and music stores became routine during my off time in New York City. My feet were still healing, but when I felt good enough I took the subway to the various Christian music and bookstores and I would spend hours there. I was usually alone. My new friends in New York were great guys, but none of them were interested in exploring or talking about the things of God. Many of these guys were Catholics, Methodists, Baptists, and various other denominations, but they were content to go to church (if they did at all) and trust the doctrine they were raised in. They saw no reason to give it further thought.

Occasionally I went back to a Catholic church. I knew more about Jesus than I did before, and you would think that would mean I had fewer questions, but that wasn't the case. More conflicts and questions arose in my mind. The purgatory doctrine made even less sense than ever, and I could not understand why Catholic priests could not marry. After all, Peter was considered to be the first pope. He and many of the other disciples had been married. What had changed?

Points to Ponder

1. Be bold with God in your prayers and tell Him you want to know His truth. A prayer like that will never go unanswered.
2. Have you noticed a direct correlation between your spiritual growth and the type of books you read and music you listen to? If so, how can you be more intentional about your choices?
3. What Christian books or music has made the biggest impact on you? Why?

Chapter 4

ESCAPING TRADITION

Therefore if the Son makes you free, you shall be free indeed.

—John 8:36

IN THE EARLY 1980s I left the Coast Guard and went home to take advantage of a paid college program for disabled veterans. I had planned on staying in the Coast Guard and advancing to officer's candidate school but my injury changed all that. One could not endure the rigors of the OCS boot camp when one can hardly walk. So for a while I lived at home with my parents and went to college. I still went to the Catholic church because I did not know where else to go. Whenever the Scripture readings were done I paid strict attention and was blessed. Whenever it was just the prayer chants or discussions about church doctrine, I got bored.

When I could, I still listened on the radio and TV to speakers such as Charles Stanley and Billy Graham. In my excitement I told my parents about my amazing underwater spiritual experience, but they were not impressed by my newfound spiritual quest. I overheard them at one point say, "He must have hit his head underwater, and he is acting so strange."

It was during this timeframe that I met the woman who would become my wife. Kathy went to the same nursing school as my sister. She had also been raised Catholic, and as we started to fall in love I knew I had to let her know my theological differences with the church. A short time later, some of her nursing friends invited her to go to a Christian concert. She had avoided their invitations to Christian events in the past, but she accepted their invitation this time because of some of the things I was sharing with her. She was touched and accepted Christ when they had an altar call. She could not wait to tell me.

We were married in 1984 in a Catholic church. By this time I was going to church as a formality since I was getting my spiritual nourishment from books and radio. The priest at the church where we got married was enlightened and easier to talk to than most Catholic priests I had met. He did not emphasize the man-made church doctrine. His homilies focused on the gospel reading that he chose.

When my first daughter, Danielle, was born, our families expected us to have Danielle baptized into the Catholic church. At the time, the church taught that if a baby was not baptized and died, it went to a place called limbo, which was neither heaven nor hell, but a sort of suspended animation state. Of course I found this nowhere in the Bible and I voiced that to anybody who would listen. I reasoned that if there was this much at stake, then the priest should be in the delivery room with the mother and baptize the baby as soon as it is born. Since the Catholic church didn't practice that, it meant they really didn't believe this doctrine. But rather, they pushed infant baptism so the child would be a Catholic and grow up as such. When I confronted the priest with this argument (the same one who married us) he gave me a wry, knowing smile and said, "Don't you think you should go through it anyway just to keep peace with your family?"

He was right. My parents were already nervous about me because of my scandalous behavior of watching non-Catholic men like Charles Stanley and Billy Graham. And yet Kathy and I had still not made the break. There were things I still liked about the Catholic church, but much more that I did not like. I believed that if I went anywhere else, I would probably find problems there too. Looking back, I think that is why we stayed in the Catholic church as long as we did. It was that and not wanting to enrage our families (more mine than Kathy's). I was fine with it for a while since we were getting fed spiritually by the preachers we had come to trust on radio and TV. Staying with the Catholic church became a formality to retain family peace. But that changed in 1987.

One Sunday morning in the summer of 1987 I was restless. We had already gone to Catholic Mass the night before to "fulfill our obligation." But I believe the hand of the Lord was heavy on me to have my family go somewhere else. I got in the car by myself and drove to Boonville, New York (the closest town) and I drove past several churches. I finally pulled into the parking lot of a small Assemblies of God church. I did not know anything about this denomination, but felt compelled to go in. I was a little late, and there were only about fifteen people in attendance, and ten of them looked like they were over eighty.

The pastor, however, was young and vibrant. I had never heard anyone speak in person like he did. He took the Scripture and made it come alive, much like Charles Stanley did for me on TV. After the service was over, I met some other people who were closer to my age (Cindy and Loren, and Wayne and Lynn). I got home and told Kathy everything.

I told her we needed to go there again next week. I found out that Wayne worked at the same place I did (General Electric in Utica, New York) and so we started to carpool. I give Wayne a lot of credit because he had to put up with my constant questions about his church. He has a quiet calm spirit about him and he was able to put up with me. Loren is someone with whom I can spend hours talking about the things of God. He likes to go deep, and I have not met many people who like to do that. He has such a positive outlook on life, even when he is going through tough times. He is a powerful prayer intercessor, and I am grateful that he has had prayed for my family for years. Needless to say, we became fast friends with Wayne and Lynn, and Cindy and Loren and continue to be to this day (Cindy went to be with the Lord in 2010).

We started having Bible studies together and continued to grow. Meeting and becoming friends with people who liked pondering the things of God together met a deep spiritual need I had all my life. It was so different than my experience with my Catholic friends. Whenever I spent time with my Catholic friends, they would ask me why I listened to Christian music or why I desired to talk to God. "That is church stuff," they would say. "Let's party!" For a short while, we kept going to Catholic Mass on Saturday night and to the Assemblies of God on

Sunday morning. But the comparison was like night and day. We would leave the Catholic church bored and frustrated, and we would leave the Assemblies of God service enriched and enthused. The amazing thing is that the Assemblies service was twice as long and I still liked it better. Miracles do happen. We had broken free.

Points to Ponder

1. It may seem safer to hide in the tradition you were raised so you don't "rock the boat" with your family. However, if Jesus begins to show you truth, pray for His strength to persevere. After all, we are to serve Him and not men.
2. Where are you on your journey? Is where you worship a place that is alive with the presence of God? If not, is it time to change churches?
3. Have you joined a Bible study to go deeper with other believers? If not, what is holding you back?

Chapter 5

THE MINISTRY YEARS

WE STAYED AT the Assemblies of God church for a year and a half. One day Wayne told me that he and Lynn had visited another local church called Abundant Life Fellowship. There were more people their age there, and there was a better ministry for kids. The pastor at the Assemblies had left, and the replacement was a great guy, but not the preacher the previous one was. The membership was still a much older crowd, and Cindy and Loren had moved to Utica and were going to a church down there. We hung in for a while, but decided we were going to try Abundant Life Fellowship as well.

I also started attending a noontime Bible study where I worked at GE. The leader liked to assign teaching responsibilities to each one of us in the group. After I had taken a few turns, he told me he thought I had a tremendous teaching gift. He invited me to go with him on Sunday nights to teach at Mid-State Prison. He was a part-time ordained minister who ran a church service for prisoners. When I drove home that night I was terrified at the thought of this. I did not see myself as a Bible teacher because I still had so much to learn. It was a Friday and I told him I would think about it over the weekend and get back to him.

It so happened that this was the Sunday we were going to try Abundant Life Fellowship. I did not tell Kathy or Wayne about the prison teaching possibility. It was really bothering me because I did not want to let Don (the leader of the GE Bible group) down. I just did not believe it was something I could do.

We walked into Abundant Life Fellowship on Sunday morning. We were a little late, so the worship service was already in progress. I was startled as the people were clapping and jumping and seemed to really be enjoying themselves during the worship. The worship at the Assemblies church consisted of the pastor with a guitar singing hymns. That was good, but this was totally different. Then came another game-changing moment.

Pastor Dan was playing guitar and singing when he suddenly decided to stop. He put his guitar down and walked out into the congregation. He headed in our direction, stopping right in front of me, and he put his hands on top of my head. Yes, I was freaked out at this point! He started prophesying. "Do not fear to go into the dark place, for where you go I will put words in your mouth and you will speak what I want you to say." I felt a power go through me from head to toe. "I am sorry if I startled you," he said, "but when you came in I saw you covered with the blood of Christ and was compelled to prophesy over you." I really needed to hear this. Ever since Don had asked me to go into the prison I had been plagued with doubts—doubts about my own salvation and doubts about teaching others how to be saved. This was an attack from the enemy of our souls, but I did not know how to handle it at that time. After this experience, I was ready to report for duty. I told Don the next Monday that I was ready to go.

I ministered in the prison for about two years. This proved to be a training ground for later ministry. I was able to teach or give a sermon every other Sunday. This taught me to prepare and study harder and it taught me how to deliver a message. The prisoners were happy to get out of the cells, so they weren't going anywhere. Some became committed Christians and we had some powerful altar calls.

One prisoner came to me and said he was awakened every night by demonic nightmares and could not sleep. He wondered what he should do. Immediately a thought entered my mind. I told him that when he was awakened, he should start praying for his family and friends. If he fell back asleep and was awakened by dark thoughts and dreams again, he should do the same thing. He came back the next week grinning from ear to ear. He said he tried it, and the nightmares stopped. I told him the enemy was not going to wake him up so he could pray. The enemy wants to torment. But since he fought back, he was being left alone. I was ecstatic about actually helping someone. But of course it was not me, but the Spirit of the Lord working through me.

This point was really driven home some weeks later as I was driving to the prison and almost turned around because I was sick. I had to go since Don was not going to be there that week and I was leading the service. I spoke the message the best I could and hoped for the best. To my great surprise, I had the biggest response I ever had. When I left that night I said to the Lord that it was all Him. What I felt the Lord impress on my spirit was that whether I felt good or bad it was always Him flowing through, that it was never going to be me. Because I had felt so sick, it was easy to understand the lesson. In any ministry effort, we are expected to give the effort, but we must always depend on the Lord to bring the results.

After the experience at Abundant Life Fellowship, we continued to go there and eventually became members. I felt bad about leaving the Assemblies of God church. With Cindy, Loren, Wayne, Lynn, and us leaving, it left the church with ten members who were over seventy years old. But with what happened to me with the prophetic occurrence, I believed it was what we were supposed to do.

Over time, Pastor Dan seemed to recognize the same teaching gift in me that Don had recognized. Eventually he asked me to teach the congregation on Wednesday nights. This went on for two years. Between this and the Sunday night prison ministry, I was getting a lot of teaching experience. I enjoyed it for several reasons. It forced me to study more to know what I was talking about, and I enjoyed seeing the light come on for people as I helped them understand. In the mid-1990s, Pastor Dan took me golfing. In the midst of the round, he told me he wanted me to become an elder in the church. I was shocked because I had never expected nor sought to be an elder. He told me that was exactly why he wanted me to become one. He was wary of people who openly campaigned for such an office. Not only did I become an elder, but a few years later I was ordained as a minister alongside another elder in the church named Brian. People started calling me Pastor Dan, which was quite strange at first. A Catholic boy had gone a full 180 degrees to become a Protestant minister. I no longer saw myself as Catholic or Protestant because I did not like either title or titles in general. I considered myself a Christian, a follower of Christ. That is what people called themselves in the early days and that was good enough for me.

Teaching on Wednesday evenings was one thing, but preaching on Sunday morning was another matter. The first few times I was quite nervous and it showed. After a while I just decided to forget what people thought and instead focus on delivering the message I believed God gave to me. Once I focused on what the Lord wanted me to say and not on me, things went much smoother. To this day when I am invited back to speak, I still get nervous the first few minutes, but once I get into the message and what God wants me to say I am fine.

For ten years, my wife and I were in part-time ministry with Abundant Life in Boonville. I include my wife because it is no easy thing being a pastor's wife, even a part-time one. We opened our home to home groups, counseling, and other meetings. I taught Wednesday nights and Sunday school. There was still the occasional Sunday morning service. As invitations to speak at other churches came in, I accepted them as well. I wrote and directed three plays as well as acted in some of them. I loved using my creative/theatrical gifts, but on top of a full-time job and a growing family, I was spreading myself too thin.

My job with Lockheed forced me to move to Syracuse in 2005. When we started attending another church near Syracuse, I trimmed my public ministry. I did some occasional Wednesday night teaching, but my travel schedule with my defense job prevented me from being consistent.

I believe the Lord takes us through seasons. If I was supposed to be in full-time ministry, it would have worked out that way. I was open to it for a time, but it never came to be. As I write this, I am in my midfifties and I look forward to teaching my grandchildren the concepts I have learned to further strengthen the path this change agent has been forging. Abundant Life still invites me back occasionally to preach on Sundays, and I always enjoy it because it allows me to deliver and teach what the Lord has been teaching me. I will always be grateful to Pastor Dan at Abundant Life Fellowship in Boonville. He saw a gift in me and encouraged me to stretch myself, even when I was uncomfortable. He is someone who truly cares for his flock.

I am open to teaching and helping at our new church as well, as my schedule allows. But as I get older, it is important to me to share what I have learned with my kids and grandkids. They are my best legacy.

I and my wife, who were both born into traditional Catholicism, are following the Lord as Bible-believing Christians. Our children—Danielle, Debbie, Kristin, and Stephen—are grown up now and following the Lord as Bible-believing Christians. Debbie is married to a man who is a bit of a change agent himself. Her husband, Joe, was born into the Armstrong movement, which was a cult started by Herbert W. Armstrong. It is basically a system that believes Israel lost out on all of God's promises and they will be fulfilled for the "one true church" (there's that term again), which is the people who believe in Armstrong's teaching (also called the Worldwide Church of God). Joe broke out of this and met our daughter Debbie at our Abundant Life Church. As of the date of writing this chapter they now have three handsome boys of their own who are being raised with a biblical point of view.

I can only look back (and forward) and feel very blessed that this change has occurred in my family line. We do not know when the Lord will return. The way the world is going, I believe it will be soon. But if it is not, I am hopeful that the faith of my family is now equipped with deeper roots. Those who are simply riding the tradition of what they were born into have no roots at all and will be subject to every vain philosophy that comes along (of which there are many).

Points to Ponder

1. Have you ever looked back and thought about how God has led you even when you did not realize He was doing so? If not, start trusting Him in little things, and when you see His faithfulness, you will begin to trust Him with the bigger things.
2. Are you approaching a new season in life? If you see God in it, embrace it.
3. If you have a deep understanding of your beliefs, you will be able to stand strong when challenged.

Part Two

REFLECTIONS ALONG THE JOURNEY

Chapter 6

THE ONE TRUE CHURCH?

> Again I say to you that if two of you agree on earth concerning anything that they ask, it will be done for them by My Father in heaven. For where two or three are gathered together in My name, I am there in the midst of them.
>
> —Matthew 18:19–20

AS A CHILD, when I asked why there were so many Protestant denominations, the answer the Catholic Church provided was that Catholicism is the "one true church" started by the apostles and that all the other churches were splinter groups that broke off from the Mother church.

With my decision to start at the very beginning of Christianity, I found more than a slightly different history.

For the first three hundred years or so after the ascension of Jesus, the early Christians were persecuted by the Roman government. They met and worshipped in people's homes and caves under the fear of being discovered. Imprisonment and martyrdom were common during this period. However, the Christian community grew, spread, and flourished. The Roman government started to realize that for every Christian they killed, several more would take their place.

In the year 313, the Roman emperor Constantine issued an edict that stated that Christians should be allowed to follow their faith without restrictions. But this came with a heavy price. As this evolved, it was accepted only in a form that blended biblical Christianity with Roman pagan practices. For example, the Romans had many gods, and some were female. So, they didn't accept a Jesus-only approach to the faith, and when they heard about the virgin birth, they began the practice of idolizing Mary, the mother of Jesus.

From what I see in the Bible, Mary is worthy of our highest respect. She obediently and humbly accepted what the angel told her about bearing the Savior. She and Joseph became outcasts and the subject of whispers and rumors about their first Child. Only they knew the truth (Joseph was told by an angel in a dream). However, they endured this and Mary had to endure watching her Son suffer an excruciating death on the cross.

It has been my observation over the years that Catholicism promotes Mary to the point of worship and being coequal to Jesus; and some Protestants have gone the other way, fearing any mention of her contributions. Both approaches are of course wrong. Scripture honors and acknowledges her faith, and we should as well.

Paganism also merged with biblical Christianity at the time of Constantine as he advocated Christmas and Easter.

We don't know the exact date of Jesus' birth, but the Scripture says that the shepherds were watching their flocks through the night. The only time they did that was during the sheep's birthing season, which is in March or April. So in reality, Jesus was probably born in the late winter or early spring. However, the Romans were big on the goddess Isis, who was celebrated on December 25. The idea of a virgin birth was a key to celebrate the birth of Jesus on December 25 because this kept the Roman pagans happy and they still could celebrate this as a feast day. I celebrate Christmas as much as anyone, but I know that this was a day that has been selected to celebrate

His birth and is not the actual day. Our society as a whole is trying to take "Christ" completely out of "Christmas" by outlawing nativity scenes and calling the Christmas holiday the "winter holiday" so as to not offend people who are not Christians. Many people who celebrate Christmas do not even give Jesus a second thought. No wonder Jesus asked (Luke 18:8), when He came back would "He really find faith on the earth?"

"Easter" comes from the word *Ishtar*, who was the Babylonian goddess of fertility. Eggs and animals that were considered fertile (such as rabbits) were in high regard. So a day to honor the resurrection of Jesus is called Easter. Of course, what is the secular theme of Easter? You got it—decorating eggs and eating chocolate rabbits. Coincidence? Not at all. In my home, we call the day Resurrection Day and not Easter. Once you know the truth about a matter, it is hard to go along with the charade.

Other unbiblical practices crept into the church over the next few centuries. "Infallible" popes initially allowed priests to marry and have families, then they decided to overturn the practice (the church decided they could not afford to pay for the expenses of families). The concept of purgatory was at first shot down, and then allowed (the church needed money). Soon the average person was not allowed to read the Scriptures because they were not deemed qualified to understand them on their own. Once this became the norm, all kinds of practices were invented by men who became coequal with and even superseded the Word of God.

Finally, in 1517, a monk named Martin Luther could take it no longer. It had gotten to the point that the rich were allowed to buy their way out of purgatory and into heaven by purchasing "indulgences" from the church. Also, once you died, it was incumbent on your relatives to continue to spend big bucks to spring you out of purgatory.

Luther had enough, and he nailed his ninety-five protests or theses onto the door of the All Saints' Church in Wittenberg, Germany. This act jump-started what John Wycliffe had started in theory some two hundred years earlier (Wycliffe has been called the "Morning Star of the Reformation"). However, Luther's bold act was the key to what has been called the Reformation or the Protestant movement—named as such because those involved at the start were officially protesting what the church had become.

Luther's followers became known as "Lutherans," and they started a path back to biblical Christianity. They did not abandon all Roman Catholic practices, and so a group who objected to infant baptism broke away from the Lutherans and became the "Baptists."

Later some people wanted to restore an emphasis on holiness and that started the "Methodist" movement.

I could go on and on, but you can see just from the above how all the denominations started. Usually people within an existing group believed there was a certain emphasis lacking and so they would start another group that focused (sometimes to an extreme) on what had been lacking.

I do believe there are some true Christians in the Roman Catholic church. But they are saved not because of their church system, but in spite of it. Any church system that teaches faith in Jesus plus (fill in the blank) equals salvation is an abomination. This is no less true of any Protestant church. There are some who think that just because they belong to a church and do good deeds that somehow that merits heaven. That is far from the truth and you can see the hand of Satan, our adversary, behind it. After all, if you want to keep people from finding the truth about the gospel, why not merge the truth with paganism and then later, when people rediscover truth, invoke arguments and wars between each other. This, of course, is the opposite of what Jesus intends His followers to do.

Do an in-depth study of Christian history and you will become more convinced that the "true church" is not some man-made organization or a building, but consists of men and women who have chosen the narrow way. Here's how Jesus said it: "I am the way, the truth, and the life. No one comes to the Father except through Me" (John 14:6).

Jesus describes salvation clearly in the above scripture. The only way to get to the Father (i.e., God, heaven, eternal life) is through Him. That makes it very narrow. You can't go thorough Muhammad, Buddha, Krishna, Hinduism, or any other ism, schism, or way. It is Jesus. That is it. His blood sacrifice paid our sin debt. When we believe and embrace that fact, it changes us. That is the essence of what being "born again" really means. You may like or dislike the term, but if you are trusting what Christ did at the cross alone for your salvation, that is what you are—born again.

When I share this with people, they often say, "That is very narrow-minded thinking." Very true. But I didn't say it. You didn't say it. Jesus said it. And if He is Lord of all, then He is right and worthy of our obedience. This is where people often say, "Well, how do you know He is the only way? Why should we trust Him and not others?" Good question; and easily answered. Jesus is the only one who taught what He did and dared stake everything He taught on whether or not He rose from the dead ("Jesus answered and said to them, 'Destroy this temple, and in three days I will raise it up'" [John 2:19]). He was of course speaking of the temple of His body. He backed this up by rising from the dead.

One of my favorite things to teach when I have the opportunity to do so is a teaching called "Proofs of the Resurrection." If Jesus staked everything He taught on whether or not He rose from the dead, is this not an important thing to probe? The good news for those who study this is that there is plenty of evidence that He did. There are several prominent people in history who set aside time from their life to try and prove that He did not rise from the dead. Within days or weeks, these people were on their knees asking Jesus to forgive them. They discovered there was enough evidence out there that would stand up in court today. I used to have to gather all this evidence from books and tapes to put my notes together to teach. Now it is all over the Internet. All you have to do is go to Google or Yahoo and type in "Proofs of the Resurrection of Jesus Christ" and you will find it all. You will find the evidence I speak of and also the stories of many who started out to disprove the resurrection and came to believe (Josh McDowell would be one example).

Once you believe, you will have a decision to make. Since He rose from the dead, He is exactly who He said He was and His teachings are validated. So getting back to the beginning of this chapter, if He says He is the only way to the Father, then it is so. If you believe as I do, that makes you, me, and

Him narrow-minded, as the world and its system likes to say.

In his famous book *Mere Christianity*, C. S. Lewis (who had been an agnostic) makes this statement:

> A man who was merely a man and said the sort of things Jesus said would not be a great moral teacher. He would either be a lunatic—on the level with a man who says he is a poached egg—or he would be the devil of hell. You must take your choice. Either this was, and is, the Son of God, or else a madman or something worse. You can shut him up for a fool or you can fall at his feet and call him Lord and God. But let us not come with any patronizing nonsense about his being a great human teacher. He has not left that open to us.

Despite whatever church I attend, I prefer to just refer to myself as Christian or "Christ follower." I realize the term "Christian" is a common expression, so I will explain what I mean by it. Read the book of Acts and the epistles of Paul, Peter, and John. You will see what life was like for the early Christ followers, and their letters share their deepest thoughts and experiences. Keep in mind that the church is not a building or denomination. It is a term meant to depict the body of believers. The true church looks to Jesus Christ for the atonement of its sin and serves

Him as Lord. They don't just mentally assent to it; they endeavor to live it and are grieved when they fail. As you study the early church, you will see that to call yourself a Christian meant putting your life on the line. There was no such thing as a casual or part-time Christian. It was, and is, a lifestyle.

One of the questions at the end of the previous chapter was about the makeup of the true church. I hope you can see now that the answer is quite simple. Whether you are Catholic, Methodist, Lutheran, Baptist, Presbyterian, or any other denomination, or independent church, if you believe that Jesus died in your place for the redemption of your soul you are saved and born again whether you like that term or not. That is what makes you a member of the true church. When we get to heaven there will not be a section for each denomination. It will be a place where our position in Christ unites us, which is supposed to be what is happening down here on earth.

Points to Ponder

1. There are many great Christian denominations. Did you ever wonder why there were so many? Go back to the beginning like I did and see how arguments and bickering caused many of them to develop. Understanding how this occurred will help you understand the denomination you were raised in.

2. Is the church you attend full of life? Are they preaching the Word of God or more interested in their own doctrines and rules? If there is life, praise God for your church and pray for the leadership.
3. Do you understand that the church is not a building or system but a group of true believers?

Chapter 7

PROPHETS AND PROFITS

> Study to shew thyself approved unto God, a workman that needeth not to be ashamed, rightly dividing the word of truth.
>
> —2 Timothy 2:15 KJV

THIS IS PERHAPS the most difficult chapter to write because I don't want to tear down what can really occur in the kingdom of God. By that I mean I believe we cannot put God in a box as some do and say that there are certain things He cannot do today. I have seen firsthand the gifts of the Spirit in operation. I have also seen them misused and outright faked. The key then is to have discernment.

There are those who teach that healings and miracles don't happen today—that they died out with the original apostles and the apostle Paul and now we have the Scriptures, and they are sufficient. Well, thank God we have the Scriptures. However, I noticed that the apostles laid hands on others and prayed the gifts into them as well. I am sure that the people the apostles prayed for did the same thing. If the gifts of the Spirit really died out, at what point did this happen?

I have read a book by John Lake (a minister who in the late 1800s and early 1900s had a strong healing ministry) whereby he states that the healing anointing was on him so strong at times that everyone was healed. Other times nothing happened. Why is this? We don't know. This happens today. I have been to services where people are prayed for until we are all blue in the face and nothing happens. Other times I have seen some wonderful things happen. It is always up to the sovereign will of God. Just because you are prayed for and you don't get healed does not mean God does not love you. It may mean that God will use your situation for His glory.

An example of this occurred in the late 1980s. Within the small Assemblies of God church we were going to at the time, there was a lady with cancer who was quite upset and sad that God had not healed her despite all the times she had gone forward for prayer. One Sunday morning she came to church and her face was beaming. She told us she knew why she had not been healed yet. She had been in the hospital that week and was in a room with another lady who also had cancer. She had been able to share the gospel with this lady and this woman received Jesus as her Lord and Savior. She died the next day. If she had not been in that room at the time, she would not have been able to witness Christ to this woman. Perhaps she is right. Perhaps it was her appointment to witness to this woman. We just don't know.

I look at it this way. We shouldn't try to put God in a box. We can go to the Great Physician ourselves and tell Him our need and ask for healing. We can also ask the body of Christ to pray for us because He often does work through His people. What we need to do is believe God can heal and then see what He does. Ultimately we are here for His divine purpose and not our own. Be expectant and see what He will do.

The same thoughts apply to the prophetic word. I have seen people prophesied over that I knew very well and the prophet was right on with his insights. I have also seen them be way off. It comes down to the fact that some people really do have this anointing or gift. Some don't and think they do. Some don't and know it and are in it just for the money (the same can be said for some "healers"). These kinds of people are not "prophets," but are in it just for the "profit." May God have mercy on them.

I am cautious when I see a sign outside a church that says "Healing Service Tonight at 7:00." If they are legit, how do they know God is going to move that way? Why not advertise a prayer service instead and then see what happens? As I mentioned earlier, John Lake was always expectant in his ministry that God would heal during a service but also observed that sometimes He did and sometimes He did not.

Another thing to consider is whether the person who is ministering is exhibiting the fruits of the Spirit.

> But the fruit of the Spirit is love, joy, peace, longsuffering, kindness, goodness, faithfulness, gentleness, self-control. Against such there is no law.
>
> —Galatians 5:22–23

Many Christians (especially some well-meaning new ones) go full throttle asking for the gifts of the Spirit, while ignoring the wonderful fruit stated above. In my experience, I have noticed that someone ministering who exhibits the fruit noted above is likely to be legitimate if he or she claims to have any of the gifts of the Spirit.

Online, you can find a lot of people who claim to be God's prophet for the end times. For example, there are some who predict there will be a huge earthquake in California. In my view, that makes you a geologist and not a prophet. The reason I say that is anyone who knows anything about California seismology is aware that a large and devastating earthquake is predicted to occur in the next thirty years or so. So to "prophesy" that a large earthquake will hit California earns a yawn from me. However, if you come and say that on September 23 at 9:00 A.M. a 7.5 earthquake will hit the San Diego area and it does, I may sit up and take notice. If you do that a few more times and you are a person who exhibits the fruit of the Spirit, I will really take notice. I do believe God still speaks to His children today. We just have to be careful who we listen to.

In the beginning of this chapter, I quoted 2 Timothy 2:15. If we study the Word of God, we are less likely to be deceived by imposters. If you do not read the Bible and have no discernment, you are easy prey for those who seek to take advantage of you. I grew up being taught that the Catholic church cannot be wrong about anything, so don't bother to question it. A lot of people don't bother to question it, so most people in it are trapped in a lukewarm state and are Bible illiterate. This of course is not just true of those in the Catholic church. There are also those in lukewarm Protestant churches as well who are simply there because for generations their family has been going there. They have never considered spiritual matters for themselves and church has become just something you do.

Points to Ponder

1. Don't ever put God in a box and think He can or can't do something just because you think so. The Bible is our guidebook. Be open to what God can do as you confirm it with Scripture. If you have this attitude, you will be able to separate the true godly activity from the scam artists.
2. Seek the fruits of the Spirit. Then ask God for whatever gift(s) He is willing to bestow upon you.

Chapter 8

POLITICALLY INCORRECT

But Peter and the *other* apostles answered and said: "We ought to obey God rather than men."

—Acts 5:29

PETER AND THE other apostles had just been brought before the Pharisees for a good talking-to. They were guilty of being politically incorrect. They were still saying Jesus was the Messiah even though the acceptable position of the day was to say He was a false prophet who had been put to death for His crimes. Peter saw the risen Christ, so he knew the truth of the matter.

Politically incorrect. That's me. That is why I could not run for office today. Some people have heard me speak at work or church and have encouraged me to run for congress in our district. Not me. Not today. I would not have a chance to get elected today (without divine intervention of course).

In my quest for truth I found out that being a Christian is a full-time lifestyle. That model is found by studying the early church Christians. There was no part-time Christianity. You stood for Christ and what He taught. Period. To do this was dangerous back then. It often meant your life.

Too often today we are tempted to be part-time Christians either when we are tempted to compromise with sin or when we talk politics. I address sin and selfishness in another chapter, so here I want to briefly address politics and more importantly being a citizen in the present world we are in.

If you truly see yourself as a Christ follower, then as much as you understand His commandments and ways, you need to adhere to them. We don't know everything and we continue to grow in Him until we die, but as much as we do know and understand we need to live it. So from studying Jesus and the Bible, I know two things for sure, and that is Jesus is not pro-abortion, as one of His commandments says do not kill, and He set up marriage between a man and a woman (Gen. 2:22–24). These are two of the key social issues of our age. If a person is running for elected office and he or she is for abortion being legal and for ignoring God's standard on marriage,

I automatically tune that person out and do not consider voting for him or her. If that person is against abortion and stands for God's position on marriage, then I will consider what he or she has to say on the economy, foreign policy, and the like.

As I have expressed this view, I have been called narrow-minded as well as simple-minded. People have told me I need to consider the big picture—that the person who is for abortion may have the real and better answers to our economy and be a better president, congressman, senator, or governor. If the person telling me this is a Christian, then he or she is not being a full-time one. I believe God can either bless or curse a nation. He either has His hand of protection on a nation or He removes it. If we honor Him by electing people who stand for His principles, He can bless our economy and solve issues we have with foreign powers. That is nothing to Him.

I believe God has taken His hand of protection off our country. In the early 1960s we took prayer out of schools. Since then we have also made it illegal to post the Ten Commandments in some places and outlawed nativity scenes in others. In many high schools and colleges you cannot mention the name of Jesus in a commencement ceremony. You can mention Buddha or Muhammad. You cannot have a Bible in the school library, but you can have a Koran.

As a result, we have lost much of our favor and blessing that this country enjoyed in the previous years of our history. Since the early '60s, we have had our president assassinated, we were tossed into a violent war in Vietnam that we could not seem to win, we have had numerous political scandals, we have had a crumbling economy, and we had the 9/11 terrorist attack, which no one thought could possibly happen here. After 9/11, the opposing political parties joined together and sang "Kumbaya" on the capitol steps. But this lasted only a few months. After that, the public prayers ended and the hatred of each other returned. As a society we have essentially told God we don't need Him. We have told Him that if He does exist, we will call on Him if we need Him. Until then, leave us alone. He is doing just that. We have lost our protection.

There is a hole in the center of our country's way of thinking. In other words, most people have no consistent purpose. The quest for information and knowledge without knowing why we even exist, combined with a war on our souls by the media and powers that be, leave us at the mercy of those who want to control our way of thinking. Unlike the time of Peter, the "acceptable position of the day" is to say it is OK for a woman to have abortions and for gay marriage to be acceptable. But God's truth has not changed, so like Peter, we must stand and say we will obey God rather than man.

Over the past few years my wife and I heard the music to the theatre productions of *Les Misérables* and *The Phantom of the Opera*. Having not seen either play, the music sounded distorted and unpleasant. However after seeing both plays we came to love the music to both. Once we knew the central story, the music made perfect sense and was quite pleasant. The Christian overtones of *Les Mis* came through loud and clear, but only after we understood the central story.

This is the problem with our current American culture. Without basic understanding of why we exist, people's political views swing from issue to issue with no rhyme or reason. In my opinion, nothing can be clearly interpreted or discerned correctly unless you understand your basic purpose/ reason for existing. People can climb the ladder and gain all the world has and still sense something is missing. The sum of what they have does not equal the whole. Howard Hughes is a perfect example. He had it all, but was miserable all the time. Something was missing. In the end, there is still a need for the spiritual and a reason for one's being.

In my search, the answer is Jesus Christ. Once I understood who He was—why He had to die on the cross and that He now sits at the right hand of the Father interceding for me, I had purpose for my life. Everything else fit within that central story. After researching the basis of many cults and religions, I found that Jesus' story was the only central story that was true. There is no other. If you grasp that as your story it will govern your life and it will spill over into your political views. As people of diverse cultures who believe in the saving grace of Jesus Christ gather to worship and fellowship, they are bound together in a way that gives them unity of purpose, despite their many cultural differences. He is the true glue that can bind us together. No amount of worldly humanism can ever accomplish that.

Points to Ponder

1. Do you find today's political climate frustrating? Press on and don't compromise your values. Someday Jesus Christ will return as King of Kings and Lord of Lords and we will forever be under His perfect rule.
2. Do you think it is OK for politicians to give a speech during which some or many of God's principles are violated and then end the speech by saying, "And may God bless America"? Is this not like your child repeatedly kicking you in the shins and then asking for a treat?

Chapter 9

ANSWERS!

> But sanctify the Lord God in your hearts, and always be ready to give a defense to everyone who asks you a reason for the hope that is in you.
>
> —1 Peter 3:15

IT WAS A cold rainy Wednesday night in the spring of 1992. Pastor Dan had asked another pastor friend of his to speak at our Wednesday night service. What Pastor Jack spoke about that night was another significant milestone in my Christian walk. He started out by saying, "Did you ever wonder if there were answers to the following questions:

- Is the earth really millions of years old like some scientists say or thousands of years like the Bible says?
- Did Noah's ark really exist? If so, how did all the different species of animals get on the ark? Was it really big enough?
- If we all come from Adam and Eve, why are there so many different races and cultures?
- Are dinosaurs mentioned in the Bible?
- Isn't evolution true?"

I was blown away by the session that night. These questions had haunted me since high school, where all the Bible stories about creation and the flood had been challenged by the science of the day. I came to understand that some scientists were actually "young earth creationists" who believed there was evidence of a young earth. Most of these young earth creationists are Christians, but many are not. The ones who are not could hardly be accused of trying to make the evidence fit into the Bible, like some say. It just shows that they see the evidence for what it is.

The issue is that most of the textbooks in schools are written by "old earth" scientists who strongly believe in evolution. Therefore, in my opinion, the textbooks are written with their slant or viewpoint. The interesting thing is that from the early 1900s to now, the textbooks change every few years. The reason is that the scientists find out they are wrong about something, so the theories change. Biblical evidence does not change. It is safe to say that man's opinion keeps on changing, but the Word of God remains true.

At the time of this writing, the theory of evolution is crumbling. But rather than believe what the Bible says, scientist are putting forth another theory that says the human race was planted here by aliens. Books such as *Chariots of the Gods* and movies like *Prometheus* push these theories along. Secular scientists will continue to do this because in their minds anything is better than believing that the God of the Bible is real.

When Pastor Jack was teaching, he told us that most of his research came from a ministry called Answers in Genesis. This ministry was started by a man named Ken Ham, who came from Australia. He was called of God to come to the United States because as a society we were embracing evolutionary teaching in the schools. He wanted to prove there were answers to our questions and that science could actually back up our beliefs. Over the years, my family and I have attended four of his seminars, and that has led me to teach the Answers in Genesis concepts to my church as well as a few others. My kids became well grounded in the truth so that when the secular challenges came at them in high school their faith was never lost. They had answers to stand on.

This is one of the most powerful challenges we have today with regard to our teens. Even in the best Christian homes, children are often taught that the story of Adam and Eve, Noah, and the Tower of Babel are just stories. When they get to junior high and high school they are inundated with secular, old earth teaching that is presented as fact. This causes many teens to question their faith and many drift away. They have no answers to their questions. In fact, they don't even ask what is on their mind because they are afraid there are no answers. When I have taught the teen class on Friday nights at our Boonville church, the teens often did not want the class to end. They would come up to the pulpit at the end and keep asking more questions. They were thrilled and astonished that there were actually questions that could be answered. We need Sunday school teachers to teach Genesis as fact by backing the stories up with the scientific evidence.

An event happened in 1981 that set the old earth crowd on their heels. The event was the eruption of Mount St. Helens. Within days there were several layers of various soil and strata that were formed for miles. If you were with an old earth scientist in Arizona and you found strata with several layers, you would point to one layer and conclude that it was fifty million years old, and another one was forty million years old, and another one was twenty-five million years old, and so on. The problem is, several layers of strata were formed over just a few days from the Mount St. Helens eruption. This is why a young earth scientist will say that the Grand Canyon was formed quickly by receding floodwaters (perhaps even Noah's flood), while an old earth scientist will say the strata at the Grand Canyon was formed over millions of years.

As far as the questions presented at the beginning of this chapter, the intent of this book is not to answer all these in detail. You can read the books of authors who can do a much better job than I can. However, I will attempt to whet your appetite for more by relating a few things I have found out and taught regarding these questions. The questions are restated below and my comments follow each question in *italics*.

- Is the earth really millions of years old like some scientists say or thousands of years like the Bible says? *From what I have studied, I believe it is thousands of years old like the Bible suggests. As stated above, the Mount St. Helens incident helped validate this. The many dating methods that are out there have been proven to be inconsistent.*

- Did Noah's ark really exist? If so, how did all the different species of animals get on the ark? Was it really big enough? *Indeed, Noah's ark did exist and there was a worldwide flood. Sea fossils have been found at the top of the Himalaya Mountains. Studies have been made and books written about the actual size and construction of the ark. There was more than enough room for each animal kind for each species. As far as how the animals all got to the ark, think of how birds migrate each year to a warmer climate. What makes them do that? The same instinct God used to drive animals to go to the ark.*
- If we all come from Adam and Eve, why are there so many different races and cultures? *Modern genetics easily proves how the races came into existence. The reality is that we all come from one race. This is a thrilling study that will answer many of your questions. All of the genetic possibilities were present in early men and women. After the dispersion at Babel, many groups went far away from each other. The dominant genes in those groups won out over a few hundred years.*
- Are dinosaurs mentioned in the Bible? *They are specifically mentioned in the book of Job (Job 40:15–24) and alluded to elsewhere.*

Recently, drawings of dinosaurs have been found in caves right along with drawings of elephants and lions. Also, dinosaur bones have been found with red blood cells intact within them. This all suggests dinosaurs were around thousands of years ago, not millions of years ago. Keep in mind, the word dinosaur *did not even come into our language until the 1800s. The words* dragons, behemoth, *or* leviathan *were often used instead.*

- Isn't evolution true? *From the many books I have studied, I say no! As noted above in this chapter, even some old earth scientist are grudgingly coming to the conclusion that the evolution theory is falling apart. Instead, they are now trying to say we were planted here by an alien race. There are many good scientific books out there to encourage you. I will say this; if evolution were true, then we humans should be getting better genetically with each generation. Modern genetics proves just the opposite. With each generation there are actually more errors and mistakes being passed on. We are not getting better, we are getting worse.*

I hope this chapter inspires you to dig deeper. There are answers to your questions. A good place to start is the Answers in Genesis website (www.

answersingenesis.org). You will find many good articles and references there. Too many people do not bother to seek answers or they latch on to what someone else has said that may be erroneous. Let that not be you. Happy hunting! What you find will be well worth the effort.

Points to Ponder

1. Don't believe everything you were taught in school. Do you realize that science textbooks change every twenty years or so as various theories and teachings are debunked and revised? However, God's teachings do not change.
2. If you really want to know truth about anything, bring the question to God. I believe He will put resources in your path to help you.

Chapter 10

THE ROOT OF OUR PROBLEMS

ONCE WE BREAK out of the bondage of thinking that our tradition or church we were raised in saves us, we are free to cling to the gospel truth that Jesus Christ is our all in all. At the same time, we need to continue to get answers to the issues and questions that plague us. This is a constant process. You may get discouraged along the way, though, as you continue to battle your sin nature.

We are born with a fallen nature into a fallen world. When we are saved or born again, we have a spirit that is regenerated to a relationship with the Father that we were always meant to have. Everything seems new because it is. We know that we have a saving relationship with Jesus, and as a result, we enjoy the things of God. We have a different feeling about other genuine Christians (we like them and want to be around them). The problem is our soul is still encased in this physical body of sin. It wants to sin—it is prone to sin. Look what the apostle Paul himself says about this:

> For we know that the law is spiritual, but I am carnal, sold under sin. For what I am doing, I do not understand. For what I will to do, that I do not practice; but what I hate, that I do. If, then, I do what I will not to do, I agree with the law that *it is* good. But now, *it is* no longer I who do it, but sin that dwells in me. For I know that in me (that is, in my flesh) nothing good dwells; for to will is present with me, but *how* to perform what is good I do not find. For the good that I will *to do*, I do not do; but the evil I will not *to do*, that I practice. Now if I do what I will not *to do*, it is no longer I who do it, but sin that dwells in me.
>
> —Romans 7:14–20

Sound familiar? It is the battle we go through once we are truly born again. Prior to being saved, we may be morally annoyed or offended by what we do because we know we have done something wrong and it bothers us. Some call this our conscience. This can vary from culture to culture. What some cultures consider wrong is perfectly acceptable in another culture. But when we are born again, God writes His law upon our hearts. Our sinful nature wants nothing of it, and the war that Paul talks about in the scripture above begins.

We are all tempted by different things. What tempts you to sin may not tempt me. What tempts me may not be a temptation to you. It is extremely frustrating to me that things I don't want to feel or be tempted by can still be a constant burden. Some Christians fight against their sin nature for a while and then simply give up. They see they have overcome some sins, but cannot fully overcome others. While it is true that Satan and demonic forces can possess a person and control him or her, this is not normally what is causing your battle with sin. Normally the root of any sin is within yourself.

Think about whatever sin you are struggling with right now and trace it back to the root. It will always end at the root of self, every time. When the pattern of the particular sin you are struggling with started, it was by something you were coveting for yourself. You focused on it, practiced it, and then it became a persistent sin. It is pure selfishness. The opposite of selfishness is forgetting about you and focusing on others. Isn't that how Jesus lived His life down here on earth? Didn't He leave His heavenly state to take on human form and suffer and die for us? He did that for us.

Charles Spurgeon once traveled a long way to preach a sermon. He was quite well known at the time and many hundreds of people had gathered to hear the famous evangelist speak. When it was time for him to speak, he rose to the pulpit, looked out at the people, and shouted the word *others* and then sat down. That was it. He was done. Some people were infuriated. They had traveled many a mile to hear the famous preacher. As mad as they were at the time, I guarantee one thing—they never forgot the sermon.

If we focus on the Lord and others, we will be less prone to give in to our selfish sinful nature. If we do fall, the Bible gives us the remedy: "If we confess our sins, He is faithful and just to forgive us *our* sins and to cleanse us from all unrighteousness" (1 John 1:9).

As mentioned earlier in this chapter, some Christians give up the fight against some of their struggles with sin and reason that "it is just the way I am." However, they end up being miserable as they are going against their new nature by giving in so easily to the old. They become a shell of the person they could be and are ineffective in the world for the Lord. If someone who is living in willful sin is not miserable, then I question whether or not he or she really had a conversion experience.

The theological debate about whether someone can lose his or her salvation has been raging for centuries. I do not think the issue is whether one can lose it or not—it is whether they ever had it to begin with. So many people get emotional at an evangelical rally or they get pushed down the aisle to "accept Jesus" by overbearing friends or relatives. They respond thinking they need "fire insurance" from hell so they "accept Jesus" and go about living how they want. This is not conversion. Real conversion is being sorry for the state you are in and feeling totally helpless. You realize you cannot save yourself and need a Savior. Not only do you want your sins forgiven, but you want the power to change. Once you understand what Jesus did on the cross, you cast all of your hope on His atonement for your sins.

Earlier in this chapter, I said we must come to the gospel truth that Jesus is our all in all. That means we trust Him for salvation and sanctification (the process by which we are changed to be more like Jesus). Too often, Christians trust Him for salvation but not sanctification. It is a daily process that continues until we die. I like the way King David put it in the Psalms: "Search me, O God, and know my heart; Try me, and know my anxieties; And see if *there is any* wicked way in me, And lead me in the way everlasting" (Ps. 139:23–24).

From what I have come to understand, David was essentially saying that there was sin in his life he was aware of, but he also wanted to know about sin he was unaware of. He asked the Lord to show him what else he needed to repent of. He wanted to be perfect before God. By this time in his life he had come to realize that his purpose in life was to be what his Creator made him to be. He was determined to fulfill that purpose.

David was called a man after God's own heart. To me, his pattern above is a good one to follow. If you want to be serious about following the Lord, you need to confess any known sin and ask for His grace to repent. No one says it is easy, but by His grace all things are possible. We only get into trouble when we believe we cannot change our ways or repent. Then after we confess and repent of all known sin, we ask God to point out sin we have overlooked or are unaware of, repenting of that as well. If we will do this on a regular basis we are in effect washing ourselves in the blood of Jesus, confessing our sins as 1 John 1:9 tells us to do, and asking Him for the grace to change.

Fight back against your sin nature. When you are under severe temptation, stop what you are doing and start praying for someone's salvation. Since you are focusing on someone else at this point and not yourself, the temptation will fade.

If you are a church leader, you should strive to raise up ministry leaders who are even more effective than you are. This goes against the grain of what the world teaches. Again, think of how unselfish that sounds. Let's say you are considered a really good Bible teacher. People really learn from you and grow because of the way you are able to teach. Now let's say you are driven to raise up two or three people to be teachers who are way better than you are. If you are successful, doesn't the kingdom of God flourish all the more? Now those two or three raise up two or three teachers even better than they. In this way the kingdom of God benefits. John the Baptist had it right when he said he must decrease and Jesus must increase. This is a kingdom principle. It squashes selfishness.

Points to Ponder

1. Selfishness is the root of every sin issue we have. Ask God to help you deal with your selfishness. Dealing with this will conquer all the specific issues automatically.
2. Can you see why striving to develop someone to be even better at ministry than you profits the kingdom of God and works to squelch selfishness?

Chapter 11

HOW THEN CAN WE LIVE?

Therefore you, O son of man, say to the house of Israel: "Thus you say, 'If our transgressions and our sins lie upon us, and we pine away in them, how can we then live?'"

—Ezekiel 33:10

Live like you'll die tomorrow and I know that you'll live forever.

—Rich Mullins

RICH MULLINS HAS been one of my favorite Christian singers since I became a believer. He went to be with the Lord in 1997, but he left behind a lot of insight and wisdom we can glean as we listen to his music. At his concerts he would say, "Live like you will die tomorrow and I know that you will live forever." Imagine if you were to live every day like it was your last day. Think how you would treat everyone if you knew it would be the last time you would see them on this earth (of course, I am assuming you are a Christian). You would not allow the cares and trials of this world to bother you at all. You would be focused only on the day you were in. Isn't it interesting that Jesus gave us this same admonition?

> Therefore I say to you, do not worry about your life, what you will eat or what you will drink; nor about your body, what you will put on. Is not life more than food and the body more than clothing? Look at the birds of the air, for they neither sow nor reap nor gather into barns; yet your heavenly Father feeds them. Are you not of more value than they? Which of you by worrying can add one cubit to his stature?
>
> So why do you worry about clothing? Consider the lilies of the field, how they grow: they neither toil nor spin; and yet I say to you that even Solomon in all his glory was not arrayed like one of these. Now if God so clothes the grass of the field, which today is, and tomorrow is thrown into the oven, *will* He not much more clothe you, O you of little faith?
>
> Therefore do not worry, saying, "What shall we eat?" or "What shall we drink?" or "What

> shall we wear?" For after all these things the Gentiles seek. For your heavenly Father knows that you need all these things. But seek first the kingdom of God and His righteousness, and all these things shall be added to you. Therefore do not worry about tomorrow, for tomorrow will worry about its own things. Sufficient for the day *is* its own trouble.
>
> —Matthew 6:25–34

I know. We are being told "don't worry." We have all heard this before. I realize it is easier said than done. I am guilty of being a big worrywart when it comes to the safety and health of my loved ones. But this is what we are to aspire to. This is where we need to ask God for more grace when we fall short.

When we step out of God's will, we should feel grieved. The Holy Spirit will gnaw at our conscience until we make things right with God. David talks in the Psalms about how he felt oppressed until he came and confessed to the Lord. This is how we know we have been born of God. He hounds us until we can take it no longer. Someone who is out of touch with God but thinks he or she is all right with Him will not have this issue. It is a sign that he or she has not truly been born again.

How then are we to live given that we know and believe it is impossible to see the world like the unregenerate do? If we understand and believe that we are here to grow in the knowledge of the Lord and live for Him as He gives us the grace to do so, it is not possible to see and live according to our old ways. We understand we are not so much living for this world as we are the next one. It is not something we turn on and off, it is our lifestyle. Early in my Christian walk, I heard a story by Dr. Charles Stanley that I never forgot. He said all humans are like caterpillars, but when we are born again we become new creations and so (just like a caterpillar) we are reborn like butterflies. A butterfly is a totally new creation. If the butterfly swoops down to join his old caterpillar buddies he will soon find out that he does not feel the same. He realizes he has new priorities of which the caterpillar cannot even understand. He no longer feels comfortable hanging around with the caterpillars—only the other butterflies. It is the same with us.

When we are born again, we receive a new nature from Christ. We can go down to the bar where we used to hang with our old buddies, but it will not be the same. We just won't feel comfortable there anymore. We are more concerned now that our old buddies change into butterflies as well.

You come to realize that you only really rest and feel comfortable when you are in the fellowship of like-minded Christians. You may find that you are more comfortable with like-minded Christians than you are with your biological family if they are not Christians. That should not surprise anyone when you consider the following scripture:

> While He [Jesus] was still talking to the multitudes, behold, His mother and brothers stood outside, seeking to speak with Him. Then one said to Him, "Look, Your mother and Your brothers are standing outside, seeking to speak with You." But He answered and said to the one who told Him, "Who is My mother and who are My brothers?" And He stretched out His hand toward His disciples and said, "Here are My mother and My brothers! For whoever does the will of My Father in heaven is My brother and sister and mother."
>
> —Matthew 12:46–50

You will only have your biological family on this earth unless they become true believers in Christ. However, you will know your Christian brothers and sisters forever.

We must live more for the next world than this one. That is totally opposite of how most people we know are living. I work at a place where (according to worldly standards) there are some very intelligent high-IQ people. They have planners and computer calendars that can tell you what they are doing six months from now as well as six minutes from now.

Yet, when you ask them where they will spend eternity, they will give you a deer-in-headlights look. Some say something like, "I guess I'll find out when I die, won't I?" The same people who absolutely need to know what they are doing for every minute of the next week are totally blowing off eternity. The enemy of their souls does not want them to even consider it.

I have come up with a story or parable that I tell people who give me such answers and it has made an impact a few times. At least it makes people think. Whenever you meet someone who is not considering why he or she needs to consider eternity, try this story:

> You witnessed a mafia murder and testified at the trial, so now you and your family need to go into the witness protection program. Authorities tell you that you will spend one week in Seattle, Washington, and then be permanently located to San Diego, California. They give you some brochures and website addresses for Seattle and San Diego so you can see what your new life will look like. Which place would you spend more time researching: Seattle or San Diego?

"San Diego," they are sure to say, since they will be there for a much longer period.

At this point you have them, as they have chosen the much longer time period. What you say to them is "So why are you spending more time consumed with the things of this lifetime? We only live here for a brief period of time, but eternity is forever. Should we not be more consumed with eternity than our lives here?"

Of course we still have to live in the here and now. We cannot put our head in the sand while here on earth. I am simply saying we need to give plenty of focus to our eternal state.

Points to Ponder

1. Do you think about the life to come or are you so bogged down with the cares of this life that you barely give eternity a thought?
2. Do you see that following Christ is a 24/7 lifestyle? We don't and can't turn it off and on when it is convenient.

Chapter 12

BEYOND THE BARRICADE

ANYONE FAMILIAR WITH the theatrical play *Les Misérables* will appreciate the title of this chapter. In these earthly bodies, we are "behind the barricade." We are trapped in these earthly vessels until we die and then we are released. Once released, we enter the spirit world—either into eternal bliss or eternal damnation. Previous chapters have noted that where you stand with Jesus Christ determines your eternal destination.

If you are a Christian, you will not face the great white throne judgment like unbelievers will (Rev. 20). This is not a place you want to appear, so be sure you have received and followed Christ as your Savior. The people who stand at this judgment will understand why they are there and will understand that their punishment is just. They will spend eternity in torment.

I think one of the hardest truths people will face here is that they will be shown the opportunities they had to receive Christ and did not do so. It is at this point that many people ask, "What about the people who have never heard of Jesus?" This is where we have to trust the Lord. The Scripture says: "Far be it from You to do such a thing as this, to slay the righteous with the wicked, so that the righteous should be as the wicked; far be it from You! Shall not the Judge of all the earth do right?" (Gen. 18:25).

I have heard missionaries tell stories of going far into the jungle where no one has ever been, and they were startled to learn that these unreached people groups have had dreams of the great God who died for His people. If someone is seeking truth, God will move heaven and earth to show it to him or her.

Christians will, however, face the judgment seat of Christ:

> For to this end Christ died and rose and lived again, that He might be Lord of both the dead and the living. But why do you judge your brother? Or why do you show contempt for your brother? For we shall all stand before the judgment seat of Christ. For it is written:

> "As I live, says the LORD, Every knee shall bow to Me, And every tongue shall confess to God."
>
> So then each of us shall give account of himself to God. Therefore let us not judge one another anymore, but rather resolve this, not to put a stumbling block or a cause to fall in *our* brother's way.
>
> —Romans 14:9–13

This judgment for believers has nothing to do with your salvation since that is determined by your acceptance of the atonement of Christ on the cross. We are, however, judged as to whether we gain rewards or suffer loss for how we conducted ourselves on earth as Christ followers.

> For we are God's fellow workers; you are God's field, *you are* God's building. According to the grace of God which was given to me, as a wise master builder I have laid the foundation, and another builds on it. But let each one take heed how he builds on it. For no other foundation can anyone lay than that which is laid, which is Jesus Christ. Now if anyone builds on this foundation *with* gold, silver, precious stones, wood, hay, straw, each one's work will become clear; for the Day will declare it, because it will be revealed by fire; and the fire will test each one's work, of what sort it is. If anyone's work which he has built on

> *it* endures, he will receive a reward. If anyone's work is burned, he will suffer loss; but he himself will be saved, yet so as through fire."
>
> —1 Corinthians 3:9–15

Anything we do for Jesus is gold, silver, and precious stones. These things will stand in the day of our judgment and we will be rewarded for our service. Any selfish acts we built on wood, hay, and stubble will burn on the day of judgment. Jesus gave an example of a Pharisee who blew a horn when he gave an offering for the poor. His reward was the attention he received at that moment. In heaven, such an act would warrant only something that would burn as it was being judged because he did it selfishly. On the other hand, when you give out of a real concern and are not broadcasting it, you are building up treasure in heaven.

So how we live as Christians is indeed important and has eternal repercussions. Think of it this way. Once you are saved by the blood of Christ by believing in His atoning death, you have a spot in heaven—a cement slab or foundation, for example. How you build on that is up to you. Don't waste your life by focusing on selfish things. What is done for Christ is all that will last. I am not just talking about people in church ministry here. Living for Christ is involved in every aspect of your life (how you treat people, your attitude toward other believers, whether you are a peacemaker or not).

At this point, you may say you are in big trouble. Remember, we can do nothing in our own strength. We must ask for His grace to live the life pleasing to Him. That in itself is hard for some people as they don't like to admit they cannot do it themselves.

As I said at the start of this chapter, one day we will break beyond the barricade of these earthly bodies. Death for the Christian is the beginning of a great new adventure. I look forward to it. Having touched death once, I am not afraid of it again, although I do fear how it may occur (I don't want to die in a fire, fall off a building, or be shark food). But the idea of having all things known to me is more appealing than hanging on to this fallen world. I cannot wait to sit at the feet of Jesus and hear teaching that is 100 percent correct. Imagine knowing the doctrines as they are supposed to be known. Imagine not having to deal with four or five interpretations of a scripture, but instead having just one meaning. I am becoming more and more frustrated to live in a world where Jesus is openly mocked—where it is OK to mention Buddha and Muhammad in schools, but not Jesus. It is more than aggravating to me that Christian viewpoints today are considered "extreme."

The real excitement lies in the concept of no more death, no more pain. I don't care how well off you may be in this world. You always know someone who is struggling with cancer or some other disease; or you know someone in severe financial distress; someone losing his or her faith; someone severely lonely; and I could go on and on. Add to this that we live in a world of much hatred (nation against nation) and a world on the brink of nuclear war. As much as I would like to escape, we cannot think that way. Jesus told us to occupy until He comes. Until He does, we must draw closer to Him and be the light to others in a world that continues to darken. We are to be His hands, His feet, and His mouth in a fallen world.

He may lead us to become a plumber, a lawyer, a doctor, a housewife, a nurse, or a construction worker, but wherever you are planted, you are to be the Lord's ambassador. You may be placed in a business, home, or other location where you are the one person who can witness to someone else by your actions or your words.

Until our time comes to join Jesus and others who have gone before us to heaven, it is fun to speculate what it will be like. We are told very little in the Bible, but what we are told is thrilling. The book of Revelation speaks of a heavenly city larger than the state of Texas. It speaks of a new earth. It speaks of us having our own mansions. It says, "Eye has not seen, nor ear heard, Nor have entered into the heart of man The things which God has prepared for those who love Him" (1 Cor. 2:9).

So we can't even imagine it. But we can try. And it is fun to do so to encourage yourself and others during hard times. I can't even imagine the joy of seeing the Lord and reuniting with loved ones and friends who also have accepted the Lord's way of salvation.

I am hopeful now that by my wife and me being change agents, our kids and their kids will have a strong Christian heritage to build on. They cannot depend on our faith because they must receive and follow Jesus on their own. But we believe that by being change agents we have made the path a little clearer to see and follow.

See you beyond the barricade!

Points to Ponder

1. Jesus Christ could return any time or you could be called home any moment. Are you ready to go "beyond the barricade"?
2. Do you now know what it means to be a "change agent"? Do you need to be one for your family?

AFTERWORD

THE SUBTITLE OF this book is *One Person's Journey from Traditional to Biblical Christianity.* My tradition just happened to be Roman Catholicism. Yours may be different. Maybe you were raised in a "dead" Protestant denomination. By dead I mean there was more focus on the church itself and not on Jesus Christ. This is not at all to infer that all denominations are dead. There are some fine ones out there that honor Christ as Lord and Savior. If that is the type of church you attend, be strong there and continue to grow. However, if you find that you were born into a church that has digressed into pure tradition, you must seek one that is biblically based and honors Christ above all.

You may be someone who was raised with no teaching on Jesus at all. I hope this little book has encouraged you to look into His life and sacrifice for us.

What I tried to do in writing this book is to share my journey and what I found out along the way. I hope it has inspired you to ask your own questions and to realize the satisfaction that comes from knowing why you believe what you believe.

—Dan Moynihan
December 7, 2012

CPSIA information can be obtained at www.ICGtesting.com
Printed in the USA
BVOW02s0057300713

327068BV00004B/12/P

9 781414 125503